# of King George V

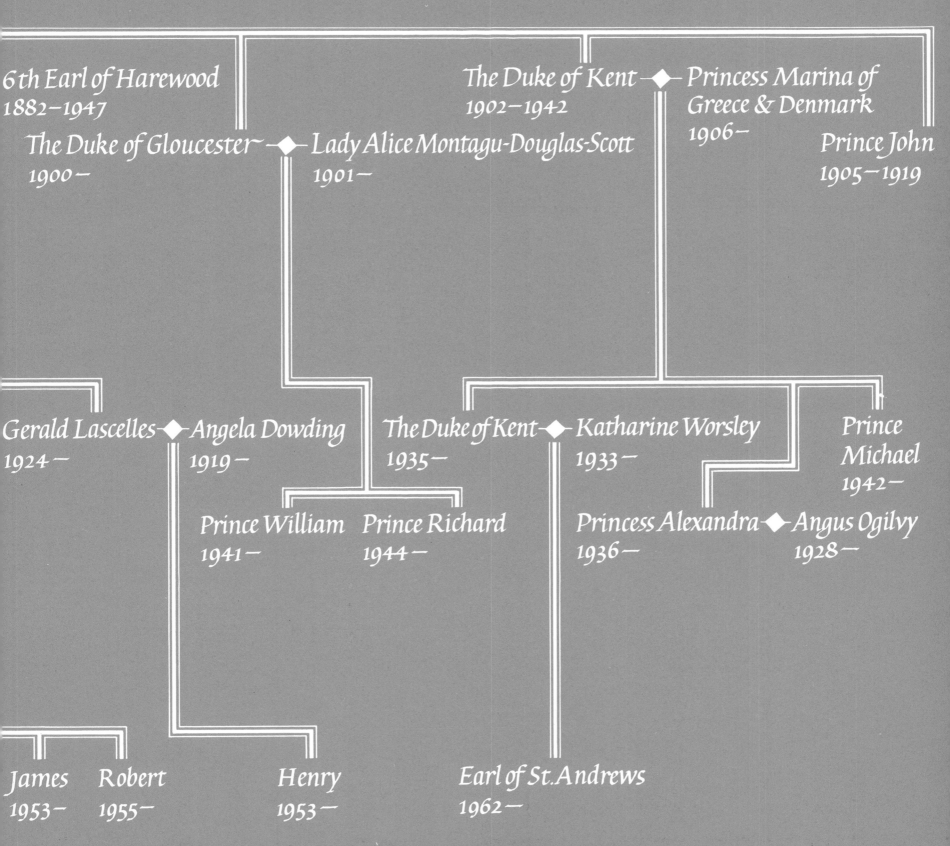

Princess Mary of Teck
(Queen Mary)
1867–1953

6th Earl of Harewood
1882–1947

The Duke of Gloucester ◆ Lady Alice Montagu-Douglas-Scott
1900 –   1901 –

The Duke of Kent ◆ Princess Marina of
1902–1942   Greece & Denmark
1906 –

Prince John
1905–1919

Gerald Lascelles ◆ Angela Dowding
1924 –   1919 –

The Duke of Kent ◆ Katharine Worsley
1935 –   1933 –

Prince
Michael
1942 –

Prince William   Prince Richard
1941 –   1944 –

Princess Alexandra ◆ Angus Ogilvy
1936 –   1928 –

James   Robert   Henry
1953 –   1955 –   1953 –

Earl of St. Andrews
1962 –

JW

Royal Portraits

Royal Portraits

BY Cecil Beaton

INTRODUCTION BY PETER QUENNELL

THE **BOBBS-MERRILL** COMPANY, INC.
A SUBSIDIARY OF **HOWARD W. SAMS & CO.**, INC.
Publishers · INDIANAPOLIS · NEW YORK

LIBRARY OF CONGRESS CATALOG NO. 62-19318

PRINTED IN SWITZERLAND BY C. J. BUCHER, LTD., LUCERNE

One of the earliest known portraits of British
Royalty is the effigy of King John which lies in
front of the altar in Worcester Cathedral

INTRODUCTION

CECIL BEATON is one of the latest in a long line of royal iconographers which stretches back to the
Norman conquest of England. For nearly a thousand years, with a brief republican interval from 1649 to
1660, Englishmen have been surrounded by the Royal image, stamped on coins, enshrined in stained-glass
windows, sculptured in the form of a sepulchral effigy or looking down from the wooden signs above
innumerable tavern doors. The first English portraits were always royal portraits; and among the earliest
and best is the impressive statue of King John, created about 1216. Supported by two small mitred figures,
the fiery and contentious sovereign lies extended before the altar of Worcester Cathedral, his crown on
his head, a jewelled collar round his neck, a massive hand grasping the hilt of a formidable broad sword.
The statue's face is clearly an attempt at a likeness—a broad, square-cheeked, imperious mask, with dis-
tended equine nostrils and a short bad-tempered nose, not the face of a man who had sought to make
himself loved, but the graphic representation of a hot-blooded feudal monarch whose craft and violence
proved his own undoing.

His son Henry III inherited his wayward character; and across the forehead of his statue in Westminster
Abbey, the noble church that he re-founded and beautified as his most enduring monument, run lines of
sorrow or anxiety that give him an unexpectedly romantic air. Just as life-like are the vivid representations
of Henry's grandson Edward II and his great-grandson Edward III—the former at Gloucester, the latter
at Westminster, respectively in alabaster and gilded bronze. Edward II, effeminate offspring of a soldier
king, has a forky beard and loose and sensual lips, while Edward III radiates solemnity and severity and
recalls a war-like patriarch of the Old Testament.

All these statues were probably derived from the wooden effigy carried in the funeral procession. The

Edward II: a replica of his
effigy in Gloucester Cathedral

The effigy of Henry III in Westminster Abbey

The effigy of Edward III in
Westminster Abbey

body itself had once been exposed; but, during the course of time, it was replaced by a facsimile, and the head was then modelled upon the features of a death-mask. Not until the close of the fourteenth century did English monarchs sit for full-length paintings. Richard II, however, and Henry V would appear to have called in fashionable artists; and Richard, who was a dandy and a dilettante, commissioned two engaging painted portraits. We see him enthroned against a golden ground, and, backed by his patron saints, kneeling before the Virgin and the Child in the famous Wilton Diptych. At the same time, he ordered a statue for his tomb—a gilt-bronze effigy executed, while he was still alive, by Nicholas Broker and Geoffrey Prest, coppersmiths of London. Few royal portraits produce so haunting an effect; the brow is high and round; the enquiring proboscis, oddly pointed; the mouth weak and rather feminine, lightly shadowed by a small moustache. Richard looks sensitive and neurotic, with an ominous suggestion of petulance and self-will.

Broker and Prest were certainly shrewd psychologists; the unknown painter who depicted Richard III was content to please his royal patron, and shows Shakespeare's 'bloody dog' as a thoughtful and dignified middle-aged man, pondering grave affairs of state and pensively turning the gold signet-ring upon his little finger. None of these statues, for all their human and historical appeal, can be considered as an aesthetic masterpiece; and the first English sovereign to employ a major artist was the founder of the Tudor dynasty. Henry VII commissioned an Italian sculptor Pietro Torrigiano, fellow

pupil of Michelangelo, to design him the splendid Italianate tomb that lies under the exquisite native fan-vaulting of the Chapel he had built to enshrine it, a monument that has been described as 'one of the most perfect buildings ever erected in England'. Torrigiano also depicted the living monarch. His coloured terra-cotta bust is the record of a royal parvenu. Its features are cold and plain and stern, beneath an unornamented wide-winged cap. Henry resembles a hard-headed businessman—he was notably cautious and avaricious—rather than an anointed sovereign, accustomed to the trappings of mediaeval majesty.

The royal look returns with his son and successor. Hans Holbein the Younger paid his first visit to England about the year 1526; and, besides portraying King Henry VIII—a huge, richly caparisoned figure, arms akimbo, thick legs wide apart, small, suspicious, cruel eyes divided by an imperious, high-bridged nose—he made a pictorial survey of the whole Court. Holbein heads the line of distinguished foreign artists who, during the next three centuries, were to help to fix the Royal image. His followers included Hans Eworth, a native of Antwerp, court-painter to Edward VI, Mary and Elizabeth I, and Marcus Gheeraerts, also a Fleming, who devoted his curious allegorical talents to the apotheosis of the Maiden Queen. Among Elizabethan artists in the royal service, Nicholas Hilliard, son of an Exeter gold-smith, was the only Englishman; and Hilliard generally confined his attention to miniatures, painted with fascinating skill on scraps of board or vellum, sometimes on the backs of playing cards.

Henceforward, the task of the royal artist was not merely to produce likenesses but to glorify and consolidate a legend. The painter became an accomplished courtier; and each artist established a type of beauty or dignity that he managed to impose on all his sitters. Our conception of Charles I, Queen Henrietta Maria and the courtly personages who surrounded them, is largely derived from the canvasses

A portrait of Henry VIII by Hans Holbein from the
Devonshire collection

of Anthony Van Dyck, whom James I had employed in 1620, and whom Charles I summoned, for a far
longer and more productive stay, in 1632. Van Dyck, a man of aristocratic temperament, did his best by
the art-loving sovereign and his Queen—in real life, Charles was a short, somewhat ill-shaped man: his
wife, a vivacious, but rather plain, woman—and then proceeded to surround them with an idealized
patriciate. His noblemen are proud, elegant, aloof; the poses they adopt are easy and languid; they have
all of them white, tapering fingers.

Similarly, it is to Peter Lely, a Dutch painter, known at home as Pieter van der Faes, that we owe
our impression of the Court of Charles II, in which images of royal and aristocratic dignity are coloured
by an atmosphere of universal licence: every court-lady's bosom is half uncovered, and nobody stands
or attempts to sit upright if it is possible to recline or loll. After Lely, the art of portrait-painting, as it was
practised about the English Court, suffered temporarily a sad eclipse. Godfrey Kneller, alias Gottfried von
Kniller, who succeeded Lely in 1680, was a comparatively uninteresting artist; and for the next touch of
genius we must await the masterly advent of two distinguished sculptors, a Fleming and a Frenchman,
John Michael Rysbrack and Louis François Roubiliac. It is they, not the painters of the age, who immor-
talized the prosaic, acquisitive society that revolved around the first Georges. True, Roubiliac steered
clear of royalty; but Rysbrack has left us memorable busts of George I, George II and the latter's intelli-
gent and erudite consort, Caroline of Ansbach. Particularly fine is his head of George II, which recalls an
incisive literary portrait drawn by Lady Mary Wortley Montagu: 'The fire of his temper appeared in
every look and gesture...'; he was naturally sincere, and his pride told him that he was placed above
restraint: he regarded 'all the men and women he met as creatures he might kiss or kick for his diversion'.

Very different was the personality of his virtuous and well-meaning grandson. At the humdrum court of George III and the chaste, but stupid and unamiable, Queen Charlotte, the only foreign artist who played an important role was the Swiss conversation-painter, Johann Zoffany. Otherwise Gainsborough, Reynolds, Romney and Hoppner held an almost undisputed sway; and, though Gainsborough produced idyllic portraits of the blooming royal children, no artist, however courtly, could have hoped to romanticise the King and Queen. George III was often painted, as a florid young man, a prosaic middle-aged monarch, a lonely and aging ruler haunted by the approach of madness. In every picture, he looks honest and serious and dull, a very decent and ordinary human being, placed in an extraordinarily difficult position.

If we except Queen Victoria's German protégé Franz Xaver Winterhalter, the last grand-mannerist to apply his sense of style to the English royal family was, of course, Sir Thomas Lawrence. The Regency and the ten-year reign of George IV provided material exactly suited to his tastes—a society dashing, showy and extravagant, with a background of martial success and steadily increasing power and wealth. But Reform now battered at the doors of Privilege; and the Court itself would soon feel the influence of commercial middle-class morality. Then, towards the end of the eighteen-thirties and at the beginning of the eighteen-forties, three great scientific pioneers, Daguerre and Niepce in France, Henry Fox Talbot in England, laid the foundations of a new and astonishing technique. They produced 'sun-pictures', primi-

tive precursors of the modern photograph; before long the industrious photographer was threatening to cut into the portrait-painter's field; and by the 'fifties the Queen herself, her husband and her children, had all submitted to this novel process. In daguerrotypes, we can examine the Queen, a solid unfashionable matron, gazing up at her tall frock-coated Consort, whose flaccid physiognomy already reveals the effects of weariness and over-work; the kilted Prince of Wales, sulky but dutiful: little Prince Albert, as the god of the vintage in a festive nursery tableau, crowned with a wreath of grapes and uncomfortably seated on a wine-cask: and the Princess Royal and Prince William of Prussia, during the earliest days of the ill-fated marriage that was to produce the future Emperor Wilhelm II of Germany.

Queen Victoria can seldom have been photographed without her full consent and knowledge. Nor was Edward VII exposed to the same hazards as are faced by twentieth-century royal personages. Although he was frequently photographed on state occasions—for example, beside President Fallières, at the opening of the Franco-British Exhibition of May 1908—during his more leisured moments he was rarely attacked by press-photographers; and, if he went shooting or attended a house-party, he sat to be photographed at the centre of a large and carefully posed group, among tweed-clad courtiers with gaiters and shooting-sticks, and wasp-waisted ladies with feathered hats and sable stoles.

Since 1914 the collapse of social barriers and the development of instantaneous photography has considerably modified the royal image, substituting for a single static representation, or a series of repre-

Queen Victoria by Winterhalter, painted in 1859 and now in the Royal collection at Buckingham Palace

sentations all based upon the same idea, a multiplicity of fragmentary impressions, here today but to-morrow dead and gone, as innumerable sheets of crumpled newsprint are swept away into the rubbish of the past. Many of these photographs deserve a better fate: they form a continuous, sometimes a moving, record of one of the best-known families in the modern world. The English Royal Family, it so happens, has inherited uncommonly distinctive traits: generation after generation, its characteristic features re-emerge. Princess Margaret as a girl was strikingly reminiscent of one of the daughters of George III painted by Zoffany and Gainsborough: and there was a remarkable likeness between the profile of her late uncle the Duke of Kent and that of his great-great-great-great grand-father, the unlucky Frederick Prince of Wales.

Cecil Beaton, as a tireless chronicler of the contemporary social scene, has long been engaged with the English royal family. This volume summarises his efforts, and displays his virtuosity in many different forms. He has a romantic side; and in some photographs the romantic element predominates. But he is also an artist with a searching eye for character; and, although his approach may be romantic, the sitter's individual qualities are never lost to view. Whereas the portrait-painters inclined to ennoble, and the press-photographer often diminishes and degrades, he pursues a steady middle path. The treatment he employs is imaginative but realistic. He shows his sitters just as they are, yet with a hint of the strangely transfiguring radiance that encircles those who occupy a throne.

PETER QUENNELL

Before the War

The Duke and Duchess of Kent
in 1935. The Duke was killed in
an air accident while on active
service on August 25, 1942

The photographs of the Duchess of Kent on these four pages were taken in 1938. The first shows her in Greek national dress

The Duchess of Kent

The photographs of Queen Elizabeth on these pages
and the one overleaf were taken in the garden at
Buckingham Palace in 1939

In the same year the following three photographs were taken of Queen Elizabeth in Buckingham Palace

The War

King George VI, in the uniform of a Marshal of the Royal Air Force, at Buckingham Palace in 1942

RIGHT: Princess Elizabeth, a portrait taken in 1942, when she was sixteen, shortly after she became Colonel of the Grenadier Guards, one of the very first public appointments which she undertook

Prince Edward and Princess Alexandra
of Kent in the garden of their home,
Coppins, in Buckinghamshire

Queen Elizabeth behind the lace
counter at a sale for charity in 1942

Princess Elizabeth and Princess Margaret at Buckingham
Palace in 1942

Queen Elizabeth with her daughters, Princess Elizabeth
and Princess Margaret, at Buckingham Palace in 1942

King George VI in 1942

RIGHT: Princess Elizabeth at
Windsor Castle in 1943

Princess Elizabeth in 1943, and RIGHT: two years later when
she was nineteen

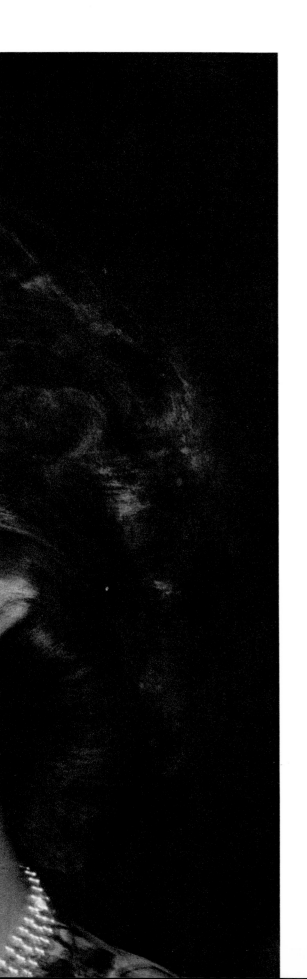

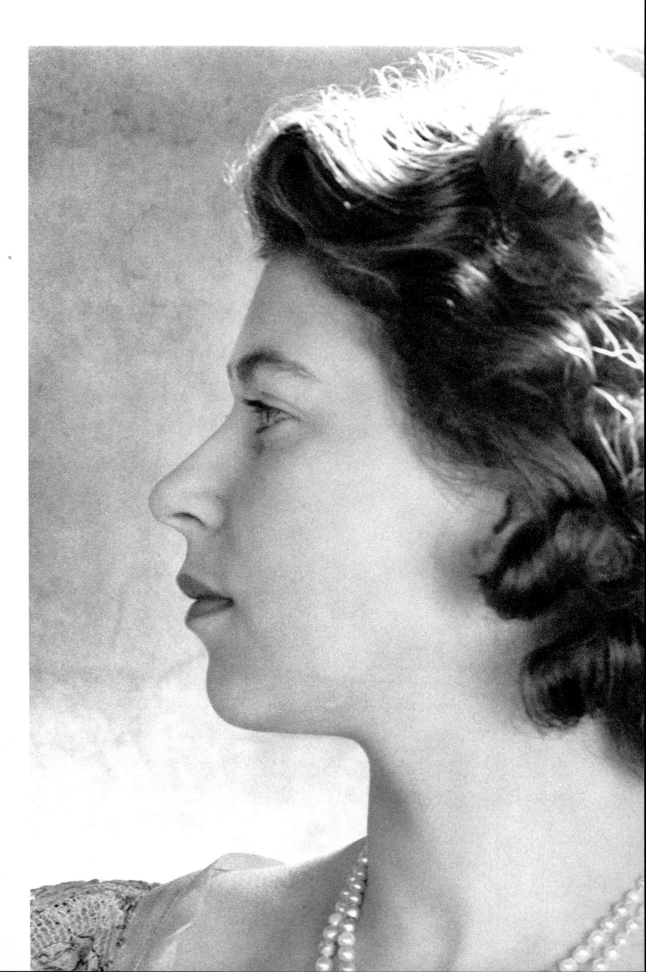

The Late Forties

LEFT: King George VI and Queen Elizabeth at Buckingham Palace in 1945

RIGHT: Princess Elizabeth in the same year

Princess Elizabeth and Princess Margaret photographed
against a wintery backdrop in 1945

Queen Elizabeth at Buckingham Palace in 1948, below
a portrait of Queen Charlotte

Princess Elizabeth with her son, Prince Charles, who was born at Buckingham Palace on November 14, 1948

Princess Margaret photographed at Buckingham Palace
in 1949 when she was nineteen

LEFT: The Duchess of Kent in her garden at Coppins,
Iver, and, BELOW: at Kensington Palace in 1949

Princess Elizabeth and Prince
Charles with Princess Anne photographed one month after the birth
of Princess Anne on August 15, 1950
at Clarence House

Princess Elizabeth
with her son, Prince
Charles, at Clarence
House in 1950.
He was then aged
nearly two years old

These two photographs were taken of Princess Margaret
on the occasion of her twenty-first birthday on
August 21, 1951

The Coronation

Prince Philip, Duke of Edinburgh and Queen Elizabeth II
at the time of her Coronation in 1953

ABOVE: Queen Elizabeth, the Queen Mother and
Princess Margaret on Coronation Day, June 2, 1953

LEFT: The Duchess of Kent with her children,
the Duke of Kent, Prince Michael and Princess Alexandra
in their Coronation robes

Prince Philip, Duke of Edinburgh and Queen Elizabeth II
on their return to Buckingham Palace from the Coronation ceremony

ABOVE: Princess Anne at Buckingham Palace on the
evening of the Coronation

RIGHT: The Duke and Duchess of Gloucester
in their Coronation robes with their two sons,
Prince William and Prince Richard

LEFT: Queen Elizabeth, the Queen Mother, at Buckingham Palace in 1953

RIGHT: Queen Elizabeth II, photographed at Buckingham Palace after the Coronation. The Black Prince's ruby is in the centre of the Imperial State Crown

Queen Elizabeth, the Queen Mother with her
grandchildren, Prince Charles and Princess Anne,
following the Coronation

The New Reign

LEFT: Queen Elizabeth II with her six maids-of-honour at Buckingham Palace after the Coronation

RIGHT: Queen Elizabeth at Buckingham Palace in 1955

LEFT: Queen Elizabeth in her
robes as Grand Master of the Order of the Garter

Princess Margaret in the garden at Clarence House
in 1955

ABOVE: The Princess Royal at St James' Palace in 1956

RIGHT: Princess Margaret at the age of twenty-six
at Clarence House

The Duchess of Kent at Kensington Palace in November 1956:
In the photograph below, she is standing beneath a portrait of her mother

Queen Elizabeth, the Queen Mother, BELOW: in 1956 and RIGHT: a year later

Prince Michael of Kent on holiday in
Florence in August, 1958

Princess Alexandra of Kent photographed before she
left for her tour of Australia in 1959

Princess Alexandra in 1959 when she was twenty-three

Princess Alexandra in the garden at Kensington Palace in 1960

The Early Sixties

Queen Elizabeth with Princess Anne and RIGHT: with Prince Andrew
photographed in March 1960 when he was one month old

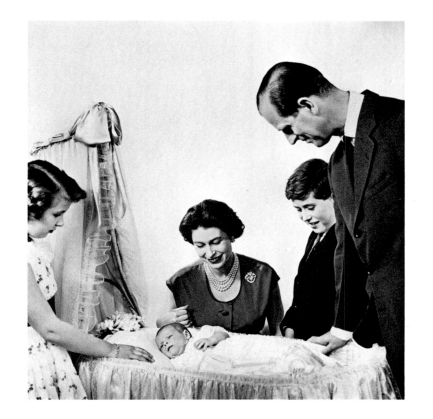

LEFT: Prince Andrew, who was born on February 19, 1960. The upper picture shows him with his parents and his brother and sister. ABOVE: Prince Charles, who was created Prince of Wales during the Empire Games at Cardiff on July 26, 1958. He was then aged nine

Princess Margaret and Antony Armstrong-Jones
at Buckingham Palace on their wedding day,
May 6, 1960

Queen Elizabeth, the Prince of Wales and Princess
Anne on Princess Margaret's wedding day. The two
children were page and bridesmaid at the ceremony

Princess Margaret and Antony Armstrong-Jones
on May 6, 1960 at Buckingham Palace

The Duke and Duchess of Gloucester at York House
in 1961. Cecil Beaton is reflected in the mirror

RIGHT: The Duke of Kent before he left for the
Independence celebrations in Sierra Leone in 1961

BELOW: Katharine Worsley after her marriage
to the Duke on June 8, 1961

Princess Alexandra, photographed at Kensington
Palace in January, 1963 on the occasion of her
engagement to the Hon Angus Ogilvy

Princess Alexandra with her fiancé, Angus Ogilvy

The Descendants

H.M. King George V
1865 – 1936

H.M. King Edward VIII ◆ *Mrs. Wallis Warfield*
(*The Duke of Windsor*)   1896 –
1894 –

The Princess Royal
1897 –

H.M. King George VI ◆ *Lady Elizabeth Bowes-Lyon*
1895 – 1952   (*Queen Elizabeth, the Queen Mother*) 1900 –

H.M. Queen Elizabeth II ◆ *Prince Philip,*
1926 –   *Duke of Edinburgh*
   1921 –

7th Earl of Harewood ◆ *Marion Stein*
1923 –   1926 –

Princess Margaret ◆ *Antony Armstrong-Jones*
1930 –   (*Earl of Snowdon*)
   1930 –

Prince Charles
(*Prince of Wales*)
1948 –

Princess Anne
1950 –

Prince Andrew
1960 –

Viscount Linley
1961 –

Viscount Lascelles
1950 –